It Could Still Be a Lake

WITHDRAWN

By Allan Fowler

Consultants

Robert L. Hillerich, Professor Emeritus,
Bowling Green State University, Bowling Green, Ohio;
Consultant, Pinellas County Schools, Florida

Lynne Kepler, Educational Consultant

Fay Robinson, Child Development Specialist

Children's Press ®
A Division of Grolier Publishing
New York   London   Hong Kong   Sydney
Danbury, Connecticut

Project Editor: Downing Publishing Services
Designer: Herman Adler Design Group
Photo Researcher: Feldman & Associates, Inc.

Library of Congress Cataloging-in-Publication Data

Fowler, Allan.
    It could still be a lake / by Allan Fowler.
      p. cm. – (Rookie read-about science)
    Includes index.
    Summary: Simple text and illustrations describe the
characteristics, origin, and pollution of lakes.
    ISBN 0-516-06051-1 (lib. bdg.) – ISBN 0-516-20072-0 (pbk.)
    1. Lakes—Juvenile literature. [1. Lakes.] I. Title.
  II. Series.
GB1603.8.F69   1996
551.48'2–dc 20   95-39662
                                            CIP
                                             AC

A lake is a body of water with land all around it.

It might be small enough
to walk around, or swim
across — and still be a lake.

Or it might be so large that people call it a sea — and still be a lake.

The Caspian Sea is a
lake — the world's largest
lake. It lies between
Europe and Asia.

The water in most
lakes is fresh water,
not salty water.

Many lakes fill low areas
that were dug out by glaciers.

Glaciers are huge sheets
of slowly moving ice.
They covered most of
our continent thousands
of years ago.

The deep ice cut into the earth, and formed long, narrow lake basins.

When the ice melted, the water filled the basins, making new lakes.

You can see why these lakes in New York State are called the Finger Lakes.

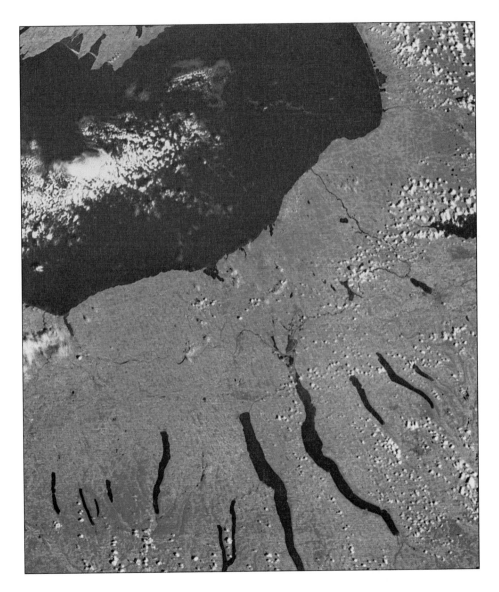

11

A mountain in Oregon
was once a volcano,
gushing red-hot lava.

The volcano died out, and its basin filled with water. It is now peaceful Crater Lake.

Not all lakes are natural.

A body of water can be created by people — and still be a lake.

When Hoover Dam was built across the Colorado River, a new lake formed behind the dam — Lake Mead.

Some lakes are great places for water sports.

People swim, waterski,
or go boating.

They fish for trout, bass, perch, whitefish, sunfish, and other fish.

Or they just enjoy the beauty of the lake.

Lakes can water farmlands.

They can give us water
to drink.

But people were often careless about lakes.

They threw trash in them.

Factories dumped waste
into lakes.

Many lakes became polluted.
Life in them died out.

Now most lakes are treated with more respect.

A polluted lake like this one could still be a clean, beautiful lake again, full of fish — with our help.

Words You Know

volcano   glacier

Crater Lake

lake

dam

factory waste

Index

About the Author

Allan Fowler is a free-lance writer with a background in advertising.
Born in New York, he lives in Chicago now and enjoys traveling.

Photo Credits

SuperStock International, Inc. — ©Tom Algire, cover; ©Edmond Van Hoorick,
9, 30 (top right); ©Peter Van Rhijn, 25
H. Armstrong Roberts — ©R. Krubner, 3; ©R. Lamb, 4, 31 (top); ©J. Swider, 17
Unicorn Stock Photos — ©Eric R. Berndt, 5; ©Robert W. Ginn, 24, 31 (bottom right)
Photri, Inc. — 7, 12, 30 (top left); NASA, 11; ©Mark Myers, 26; ©Wallis, 29
Root Resources — ©Kenneth W. Fink, 8; ©Larry Schaefer, 19
Tony Stone Images, Inc. — ©James Balog, 13, 30 (bottom); ©Peter/Stef Lamberti, 15,
31 (bottom left); ©John Lamb, 20; ©Mark Lewis, 23; ©Robert E. Daemmrich, 27
David G. Houser — ©Jan Butchofsky-Houser, 16
©Greg Ryan-Sally Beyer, 18
Photo Edit — ©Prettyman, 21
COVER: Lake Michigan